Murphy's Law Book Two

more reasons why things go ƃuoɹʍ!

D0063455

Arthur Bloch

PRICE/STERN/SLOAN
Publishers, Inc., Los Angeles
1982

ACKNOWLEDGEMENTS AND PERMISSIONS

Grateful acknowledgement is made to the following for permission to reprint
their material:

Matz's Laws, Mottos, etc.; Barach's Rule; Bernstein's Precept; Cochrane's
Aphorism; Lord Cohen's Comment; Loeb's Laws of Medicine; Shum-
way's Law: *New York State Journal of Medicine*, copyright by the
Medical Society of the State of New York, "Principles of Medicine"
(Jan. 1977) and "More Principles of Medicine" (Oct. 1977) by Robert
Matz, M.D.

Shedenhelm's Laws of Backpacking: Shedenhelm, W.R.C.; *The Backpacker's
Guide*, Mountain View, World Publications, 1979.

Herblock's Law: Block, Herbert; *Herblock's State of the Union*, NY, Simon
& Schuster, 1972.

Alinsky's Rule for Radicals: Alinsky, Saul; *Rules for Radicals*, NY, Random
House, Inc, 1971.

Kamin's Third Law: *L.A. Herald Examiner*, Dec. 2, 1973.

Glogg's Law: *National Review* (150 East 35th St., New York, NY, 10016),
Mar. 29, 1974.

FIFTH PRINTING – JANUARY 1982

ILLUSTRATED BY ED POWERS

Library of Congress Catalog Card Number: 80-80039

ISBN: 0-8431-0674-3

PSS!® is a registered trademark of Price/Stern/Sloan Publishers, Inc.

Ballance's Law of Relativity; Ballance's Law of Pragmatic Passion: *Bill Ballance's Hip Handbook of Nifty Moves*; Melvin Powers-Wilshire Book Co., 12015 Sherman Rd., N. Hollywood, CA 91605.

The Guppy Law: by Fred Reed, from *The Washington Post*, Washington, DC, June 27, 1978.

Price's Laws: Price, Roger; *The Great Roob Revolution*, NY, Random House, Inc., 1970.

Telesco's Laws of Nursing: *American Journal of Nursing*, Dec, 1978, Vol. 78, No. 12.

Thumb's First and Second Postulates: *Nuclear News*, Aug. 1971.

Alice Hammond's Laws of the Kitchen; Working Cooks Laws; Cooper's Rule for Copying Recipes: *Randolph Guide* and *Greensboro Record*, Mar. 8, 1978.

Law of Revelation; Evans' Law: *Dukengineer*, October, 1974.

Murray's Rules of the Arena: Jim Murray's Column, L.A. Times, Nov. 23, 1978.

Dedera's Law: Jack Smith's Column, L.A. Times, Nov. 10, 1976.

Four Workshop Principles; Five Laws of Office Murphology; Eight Laws of Kitchen Confusion; Laws of Class Scheduling; Laws of Applied Terror: *Murphy's Law(s) Plaques for the Workshop; for the Office; for the Kitchen; for Students*; Copyright 1978, Arthur Bloch, published by Price/Stern/Sloan, Inc.

Borkowski's Law; Hart's Law of Observation; Law of Probable Dispersal: *Verbatim*, Copyright 1977. Used by permission.

Systemantics chapter: Gall, John, M.D.; *Systemantics: How Systems Work and Especially How They Fail*; reprinted by permission of Times Books, New York, 1977.

Hofstedt's Law; Horngren's Observation; MacDonald's First and Second Laws: *Alumni Bulletin*, Stanford School of Business, Vol. 46, No. 3.

CONTENTS

PREFACE

"If I travelled to the end of the rainbow
As Dame Fortune did intend,
Murphy would be there to tell me,
The pot's at the other end."

— Bert Whitney, gentle reader.

Gentle readers:

This volume is a tribute to all who responded to the request for new Laws in *Murphy's Law I*. Since the publication of that book I have been *literally* overwhelmed with penetrating insights into the operation of the real world (the one with people in it).

The problem which I have had to face was anticipated by a correspondent from Ann Arbor, who casually stepped on my line to offer DIGIOVANNI'S LAW: "The number of Laws will expand to fill the publishing space available."

And a further process comment arrived in the form of LEO ROGERS' BLESSING FOR VOLUME II: "If it's worth doing, it's worth overdoing."

You will find this new book to be far more diversified than any collection published previously. While a small part of the contents was penned by your editor, the better portion (and the lion's share) of the Laws herein were contributed by regular folk, people just like you, only not as sensitive, who read Murphy's Law I and were inspired by THE FIFTH (and only) RULE: "You have taken yourself too seriously."

Arthur Bloch
Berkeley, California
January, 1980

INTRODUCTION

In October, 1977 the existence of an already full-blown but previously undocumented body of theory called Murphology was revealed to an unsuspecting populace in our first volume, *Murphy's Law and Other Reasons Why Things Go Wrong*. Since then, hundreds of closet Murphologists have come forth to proclaim their support for the basic tenets and to add their two cents' worth, while Murphology's place in the history of philosophical movements has been all but assured by the vociferous emergence of dissident camps, rival theories and powerfully placed pooh-poohers.

A small number of people have raised objection to Murphy's Law on the grounds that it is antithetical to our time-honored belief in the glory of Positive Thinking. My feeling is that any such tendency to identify Murphy's Law with pessimism and negativity is at best short-sighted and at worst (i.e. probably) a symptom of a deep-seated misapprehension.

For it is not in terms of our position on the optimism/pessimism scale that we Murphologists are to be understood. Despite first impressions, the Laws themselves do not represent either predisposition. The key to their transcendant philosophical nature is concealed in the notion of a thing "going wrong," which verbal construct should not

9

be construed as suggesting that "right" and "wrong" are objective entities and not subjective postures.

The accomplished Murphologist's stance is best expressed in the CARDINAL CONUNDRUM:

> *The Optimist believes we live in the best of all possible worlds.*
>
> *The Pessimist fears this is true.*

In the previous book, in a fit of glib coinage, I named one of the chapters "Applied Murphology." It has since dawned on me that this was a misnomer, and that what was meant was more on the order of "Murphology of Everyday Life" or, if you will, "Situational Murphology." While the difference may seem insignificant, it is based on the profound realization that the Murphic group of laws, by their very nature, *are unapplicable in any practical sense.* That is, when you try to use them, based on past observations of how they operate, they don't work.

No simple demonstration of this is possible. You might, it seems, try changing lines (or lanes) when the one you are in is moving slowly, to ascertain whether the new line slows appreciably when you get there. Similarly, you might try washing your car with the express purpose of causing it to rain. Unfortunately, the very fact that you are performing these actions for experimental purposes, and not because of a genuine, instinctive desire to achieve a specific outcome, will throw a monkey wrench into the already complex Murphological machinations.

Jerry Silverman, an advanced Murphologist from Berkeley, whose grasp of the situation is years ahead of his time, stated the case most succinctly when he commented:

If Murphy's Law can go wrong, it will.

To place Murphology in its broader societal context, it helps to observe that most laws fall into two groups: a) the laws of government, business and other conspiratorial human groupings; and b) the Laws of Nature.

The Laws in this book differ fundamentally from the official proclamations, legal restrictions and other "laws of men"—mainly, they differ in that no one has anything to gain by enacting Murphy-type Laws (the present struggling writer excepted).

Our Laws are more closely akin to the Natural Laws to which scientists and other tool-using, fund-seeking and axe-grinding bipeds have habitually laid claim. Indeed, they represent the failure of the scientistic method to explain the world of human experience.

The main difference between the Laws of Murphology and those of the "proper" sciences (i.e. those that pay), as we pointed out earlier, is in their relative applicability. This is expressible in terms of *predictive potential*, which in Murphy's case is zilch. The Natural Laws, those which govern physical cause and effect phenomena, are useful in predicting the results of physical interactions, and so are granted societal kudos. The Unnatural Laws, Murphy's being the generalized version, deal with intention and purpose, factors which are not physical in nature. We thus have to look elsewhere than to predictive accuracy for these Laws' value to society.

And where else to look, when prediction has failed us, but to retrospection. "Hindsight," FAGIN'S RULE reminds us, "is an exact science."

Whether we suffer from regret (over things we didn't do) or remorse (over things we did), every once in a while we will smile when things go wrong just because smiling is more important than things. And for this outlook, if for nothing else, we can thank Murphy's Law.

But lest we become over-complacent, smug in our assurance that, from now on, when things go right, "fine," and when they go wrong, "groovy," allow me to offer this Meta-Law for consideration.

THE LAST LAW:

> *If several things that could have gone wrong have not gone wrong, it would have been ultimately beneficial for them to have gone wrong.*

ADVANCED MURPHOLOGY

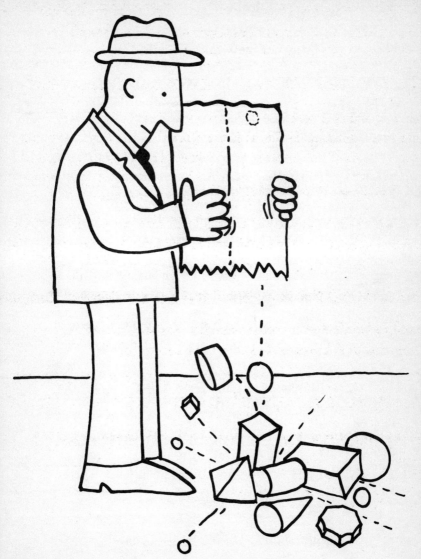

MURPHY'S LAW:

> If anything can go wrong, it will.

SCHNATTERLY'S SUMMING UP OF THE COROLLARIES:

> If anything can't go wrong, it will.

SILVERMAN'S PARADOX:

> If Murphy's Law can go wrong, it will.

THE EXTENDED MURPHY'S LAW:

> If a series of events can go wrong, it will do so in the worst possible sequence.

FARNSDICK'S COROLLARY TO THE FIFTH COROLLARY:

> After things have gone from bad to worse, the cycle will repeat itself.

GATTUSO'S EXTENSION OF MURPHY'S LAW:

> Nothing is ever so bad that it can't get worse.

LYNCH'S LAW:

> When the going gets tough, everyone leaves.

EVANS' AND BJORN'S LAW:

No matter what goes wrong, there is always somebody who knew it would.

BENEDICT'S PRINCIPLE (formerly Murphy's Ninth Corollary):

Nature always sides with the hidden flaw.

LAW OF REVELATION

The hidden flaw never remains hidden.

LANGSAM'S LAWS:

1. Everything depends.
2. Nothing is always.
3. Everything is sometimes.

HELLRUNG'S LAW:

If you wait, it will go away.
Shavelson's Extension:
. . . having done it's damage.
Grelb's Addition:
If it was bad, it'll be back.

GROSSMAN'S MISQUOTE OF H. L. MENCKEN:

Complex problems have simple, easy-to-understand wrong answers.

DUCHARME'S PRECEPT:

Opportunity always knocks at the least opportune moment.

FLUGG'S LAW:

When you need to knock on wood is when you realize the world's composed of aluminum and vinyl.

IMBESI'S LAW OF THE CONSERVATION OF FILTH:

In order for something to become clean, something else must become dirty.

Freeman's Extension:

. . . but you can get everything dirty without getting anything clean.

FIRST POSTULATE OF ISO-MURPHISM:

Things equal to nothing else are equal to each other.

BOOB'S LAW (from *Murphy's Law*):

You always find something the last place you look.

LAW OF THE SEARCH:

The first place to look for anything is the last place you would expect to find it.

MARYANN'S LAW

You can always find what you're not looking for.

RUNE'S RULE:

If you don't care where you are, you ain't lost.

COIT-MURPHY'S STATEMENT ON THE POWER OF NEGATIVE THINKING:

It is impossible for an optimist to be pleasantly surprised.

FERGUSON'S PRECEPT:

A crisis is when you can't say "let's forget the whole thing."

THE UNAPPLICABLE LAW:

Washing your car to make it rain doesn't work.

MURPHY'S SAVING GRACE:

The worst is enemy of the bad.

THE CARDINAL CONUNDRUM:

An optimist believes we live in the best of all possible worlds.

A pessimist fears this is true.

NAESER'S LAW:

You can make it foolproof, but you can't make it damnfoolproof.

SITUATIONAL
MURPHOLOGY

DRAZEN'S LAW OF RESTITUTION:

The time it takes to rectify a situation is inversely proportional to the time it took to do the damage.

Example #1:
It takes longer to glue a vase together than to break one.

Example #2:
It takes longer to lose 'X' number of pounds than to gain 'X' number of pounds.

CAFETERIA LAW:

The item you had your eye on the minute you walked in will be taken by the person in front of you.

ETORRE'S OBSERVATION (from *Murphy's Law*):

The other line moves faster.

O'BRIEN'S VARIATION ON ETORRE'S OBSERVATION:

If you change lines, the one you just left will start to move faster than the one you are now in.

Kenton's Corollary:
Switching back screws up both lines and makes everybody angry.

THE QUEUE PRINCIPLE:

The longer you wait in line, the greater the likelihood that you are standing in the wrong line.

Flugg's Rule:

The slowest checker is always at the quick-check-out lane.

WITTEN'S LAW:

Whenever you cut your fingernails you will find a need for them an hour later.

REVEREND CHICHESTER'S LAWS:

1. If the weather is extremely bad, church attendance will be down.

2. If the weather is extremely good, church attendance will be down.

3. If the bulletin covers are in short supply, church attendance will exceed all expectations.

HUTCHISON'S LAW:

If a situation requires undivided attention, it will occur simultaneously with a compelling distraction.

FULLER'S LAW OF JOURNALISM:

The further away the disaster or accident occurs, the greater the number of dead and injured required for it to become a story.

LAWS OF TRUTH IN REPORTING:

1. The closer you are to the facts of a situation, the more obvious are the errors in all news coverage of the situaion.

2. The further you are from the facts of a situation, the more you tend to believe news coverage of the situation.

THE LAW OF THE LETTER:

The best way to inspire fresh thoughts is to seal the letter.

JONES' LAW OF ZOOS AND MUSEUMS:

The most interesting specimen will not be labeled.

JONES' LAW OF PUBLISHING:

Some errors will always go unnoticed until the book is in print.

Bloch's Corollary:
The first page the author turns to upon receiving an advance copy will be the page containing the worst error.

WALLACE WOOD'S RULE OF DRAWING:

1. Never draw what you can copy.

2. Never copy what you can trace.

3. Never trace what you can cut out and paste down.

PHOTOGRAPHER'S LAWS:

1. The best shots happen immediately after the last frame is exposed.

2. The other best shots are generally attempted through the lens cap.

3. Any surviving best shots are ruined when someone inadvertently opens the darkroom door and all of the dark leaks out.

DEDERA'S LAW:

In a three-story building served by one elevator, nine times out of ten the elevator car will be on a floor where you are not.

SIR WALTER'S LAW:

The tendency of smoke from a cigarette, barbeque, campfire, etc. to drift into a person's face varies directly with that person's sensitivity to smoke.

KAUFFMAN'S FIRST LAW OF AIRPORTS:

The distance to the gate is inversely proportional to the time available to catch your flight.

ROGERS' LAW:

As soon as the stewardess serves the coffee, the airliner encounters turbulence.

Davis' Explanation of Rogers' Law:

Serving coffee on aircraft causes turbulence.

BASIC BAGGAGE PRINCIPLE:

Whatever carrousel you stand by, your baggage will come in on another one.

ANGUS' EXCHANGE AXIOM:

When travelling overseas, the exchange rate improves markedly the day after one has purchased foreign currency.

Corollary:

Upon returning home, the rate drops again as soon as one has converted all unused foreign currency.

HIERARCHIOLOGY & COMMITTOLOGY

PERKINS' POSTULATE:

The bigger they are, the harder they hit.

HARRISON'S POSTULATE:

For every action, there is an equal and opposite criticism.

ROGERS' RULE:

Authorization for a project will be granted only when none of the authorizers can be blamed if the project fails but when all of the authorizers can claim credit if it succeeds.

MOLLISON'S BUREAUCRACY HYPOTHESIS:

If an idea can survive a bureaucratic review and be implemented, it wasn't worth doing.

BACHMAN'S INEVITABILITY THEOREM:

The greater the cost of putting a plan into operation, the less chance there is of abandoning the plan — even if it subsequently becomes irrevelant.

Corollary:
The higher the level of prestige accorded the people behind the plan, the least less chance there is of abandoning it.

CONWAY'S LAW:

In any organization there will always be one person who knows what is going on.

This person must be fired.

STEWART'S LAW OF RETROACTION:

It is easier to get forgiveness than permission.

LOFTUS' THEORA ON PERSONNEL RECRUITMENT:

1. Far-away talent always seems better than home-developed talent.
2. Personnel recruiting is a triumph of hope over experience.

LOFTUS' FIFTH LAW OF MANAGEMENT:

Some people manage by the book, even though they don't know who wrote the book or even what book.

FIRST RULE OF SUPERIOR INFERIORITY:

Don't let your superiors know you're better than they are.

WHISTLER'S LAW:

You never know who's right, but you always know who's in charge.

SPENCER'S LAWS OF DATA:

1. Anyone can make a decision given enough facts.

2. A good manager can make a decision without enough facts.

3. A perfect manager can operate in perfect ignorance.

GOTTLIEB'S RULE:

The boss who attempts to impress employees with his knowledge of intricate details has lost sight of his final objective.

FIRST RULE OF NEGATIVE ANTICIPATION:

You will save yourself a lot of needless worry if you don't burn your bridges until you come to them.

PRIMARY PRINCIPLE OF SOCIO-ECONOMICS:

In a hierarchical system, the rate of pay varies inversely with the unpleasantness and difficulty of the task.

DREW'S LAW OF PROFESSIONAL PRACTICE:

The client who pays the least complains the most.

COHN'S LAW:

In any bureaucracy, paperwork increases as you spend more and more time reporting on the less and less you are doing. Stability is achieved when you spend all of your time reporting on the nothing you are doing.

MacDONALD'S SECOND LAW:

Consultants are mystical people who ask a company for a number and then give it back to them.

DINGLE'S LAW:

When somebody drops something, everybody will kick it around instead of picking it up.

KUSHNER'S LAW:

The chances of anybody doing anything are inversely proportional to the number of other people who are in a position to do it instead.

PFEIFER'S PRINCIPLE:

Never make a decision you can get someone else to make.

Corollary:
No one keeps a record of decisions you could have made but didn't. Everyone keeps a record of your bad ones.

THAL'S LAW:

For every vision, there is an equal and opposite revision.

JOE'S LAW:

The inside contact that you have developed at great expense is the first person to be let go in any reorganization.

MacDONALD'S FIRST LAW:

It's tough to get reallocated when you're the one who's redundant.

LAW OF PROBABLE DISPERSAL:

Whatever hits the fan will not be evenly distributed.

LUPOSCHAINSKY'S HURRY-UP-AND-WAIT PRINCIPLE:

If you're early, it'll be cancelled.
If you knock yourself out to be on time, you will have to wait.
If you're late, you will be too late.

GOURD'S AXIOM:

A meeting is an event at which the minutes are kept and the hours are lost.

MATILDA'S LAW OF SUB-COMMITTEE FORMATION:

If you leave the room, you're elected.

WELLINGTON'S LAW OF COMMAND:

The cream rises to the top.
So does the scum.

WORKMANSHIP & OFFICE MURPHOLOGY

HARDIN'S LAW:

You can never do just one thing.

HECHT'S FOURTH LAW:

There's no time like the present for postponing what you don't want to do.

GROSSMAN'S LEMMA:

Any task worth doing was worth doing yesterday.

KNAGG'S DERIVATIVE OF MURPHY'S LAW:

The more complicated and grandiose the plan, the greater the chance of failure.

DEHAY'S AXIOM:

Simple jobs always get put off because there will be time to do them later.

WETHERN'S LAW OF SUSPENDED JUDGMENT:

Assumption is the mother of all screw-ups.

THE EINSTEIN EXTENSION OF PARKINSON'S LAW:

A work project expands to fill the space available.

Corollary:
No matter how large the work space, if two projects must be done at the same time they will require the use of the same part of the work space.

FOUR WORKSHOP PRINCIPLES:

1. The one wrench or drill bit you need will be the one missing from the tool chest.

2. Most projects require three hands.

3. Leftover nuts never match leftover bolts.

4. The more carefully you plan a project, the more confusion there is when something goes wrong.

RAY'S RULE FOR PRECISION:

Measure with a micrometer.

Mark with chalk.

Cut with an axe.

FIRST LAW OF REPAIR:

You can't fix it if it ain't broke.

FIRST RULE OF INTELLIGENT TINKERING:

Save all the parts.

SMITH'S LAW OF COMPUTER REPAIR:

Access holes will be ½″ too small.

Corollary:
Holes that are the right size will be in the wrong place.

JARUK'S SECOND LAW:

If it would be cheaper to buy a new unit, the company will insist upon repairing the old one.

Corollary:
If it would be cheaper to repair the old one, the company will insist on the latest model.

GORE'S LAWS OF DESIGN ENGINEERING:

1. The primary function of the design engineer is to make things difficult for the fabricator and impossible for the serviceman.

2. That component of any circuit which has the shortest service life will be placed in the least accessible location.

3. Any circuit design must contain at least one part which is obsolete, two parts which are unobtainable and three parts which are still under development.

Corollaries:
1. The project engineer will change the design to suit the state-of-the-art.

2. The changes will not be mentioned in the service manual.

SIX LAWS OF OFFICE MURPHOLOGY:

1. Important letters which contain no errors will develop errors in the mail.

Corollary:
Corresponding errors will show up in the duplicate while the Boss is reading it.

2. Office machines which function perfectly during normal business hours will break down when you return to the office at night to use them for personal business.

3. Machines that have broken down will work perfectly when the repairman arrives.

4. Envelopes and stamps which don't stick when you lick them will stick to other things when you don't want them to.

5. Vital papers will demonstrate their vitality by spontaneously moving from where you left them to where you can't find them.

6. The last person who quit or was fired will be held responsible for everything that goes wrong — until the next person quits or is fired.

DEVRIES' DILEMMA:

If you hit two keys on the typewriter, the one you don't want hits the paper.

THEORY OF SELECTIVE SUPERVISION:

The one time in the day that you lean back and relax is the one time the Boss walks through the office.

ADVANCED RESEARCHMANSHIP

FIRST LAW OF LABORATORY WORK

Hot glass looks exactly the same as cold glass.

GROUND RULE FOR LABORATORY WORKERS:

When you do not know what you are doing, do it neatly.

FINAGLE'S EIGHTH RULE:

Teamwork is essential. It allows you to blame someone else.

FINAGLE'S CREED:

Science is true. Don't be misled by facts.

HANDY GUIDE TO MODERN SCIENCE:

1. If it's green or it wriggles, it's biology.

2. If it stinks, it's chemistry.

3. If it doesn't work, it's physics.

MUENCH'S LAW:

Nothing improves an innovation like lack of controls.

MAY'S LAW OF STRATIGRAPHY:

The quality of correlation is inversely proportional to the density of control.

VESILIND'S LAWS OF EXPERIMENTATION:

1. If reproducibility may be a problem, conduct the test only once.

2. If a straight line fit is required, obtain only two data points.

LERMAN'S LAW OF TECHNOLOGY:

Any technical problem can be overcome given enough time and money.

Lerman's Corollary:

You are never given enough time or money.

ROCKY'S LEMMA OF INNOVATION PREVENTION:

Unless the results are known in advance, funding agencies will reject the proposal.

THUMB'S FIRST POSTULATE:

It is better to solve a problem with a crude approximation and know the truth, $\pm 10\%$, than to demand an exact solution and not know the truth at all.

THUMB'S SECOND POSTULATE:

An easily-understood, workable falsehood is more useful than a complex, incomprehensible truth.

JONES' FIRST LAW:

Anyone who makes a significant contribution to any field of endeavor, and stays in that field long enough, becomes an obstruction to its progress — in direct proportion to the importance of his original contribution.

MANN'S LAW (generalized):

If a scientist uncovers a publishable fact, it will become central to his theory.

Corollary:
His theory, in turn, will become central to all scientific thought.

THE RULER RULE:

There is no such thing as a straight line.

GRELB'S LAW OF ERRORING:

In any series of calculations, errors tend to occur at the opposite end to the end at which you begin checking for errors.

ROBERTS' AXIOM:

Only errors exist.

Berman's Corollary to Roberts' Axiom:
One man's error is another man's data.

FIFTH LAW OF UNRELIABILITY:

To err is human, but to really foul things up requires a computer.

GREER'S THIRD LAW:

A computer program does what you tell it to do, not what you want it to do.

LEO BEISER'S FIRST COMPUTER AXIOM:

When putting it into memory, remember where you put it.

STEINBACH'S GUIDELINE FOR SYSTEMS PROGRAMMING:

Never test for an error condition you don't know how to handle.

STATE.MAN.'HIP &
ECONO-MURPHOLOGY

LIEBERMAN'S LAW:

Everybody lies; but it doesn't matter, since nobody listens

THE SAUSAGE PRINCIPLE:

People who love sausage and respect the law should never watch either one being made.

TODD'S FIRST TWO POLITICAL PRINCIPLES:

1. No matter what they're telling you, they're not telling you the whole truth.
2. No matter what they're talking about, they're talking about money.

THE WATERGATE PRINCIPLE:

Government corruption is always reported in the past tense.

ALINSKY'S RULE FOR RADICALS:

Those who are most moral are farthest from the problem.

MILES' LAW:

Where you stand depends on where you sit.

LEE'S LAW:

In any dealings with a collective body of people, the people will always be more tacky than originally expected.

EVANS' LAW:

If you can keep your head when all about you are losing theirs, then you just don't understand the problem.

RULE OF DEFACTUALIZATION:

Information deteriorates upward through bureaucracies.

RUSK'S LAW OF DELEGATION:

Where an exaggerated emphasis is placed upon delegation, responsibility, like sediment, sinks to the bottom.

THE GUPPY LAW:

When outrageous expenditures are divided finely enough, the public will not have enough stake in any one expenditure to squelch it.

Corollary:
Enough guppies can eat a treasury.

GOOD'S RULE FOR DEALING WITH BUREAUCRACIES:

When the government bureau's remedies do not match your problem, you modify the problem, not the remedy.

MARKS' LAW OF MONETARY EQUALIZATION:

A fool and your money are soon partners.

HEISENBERG PRINCIPLE OF INVESTMENT:

You may know where the market is going, but you can't possibly know where it's going after that.

HORNGREN'S OBSERVATION:

Among economists, the real world is often a special case.

SPENCER'S LAWS OF ACCOUNTANCY:

1. Trial balances don't.
2. Working capital doesn't.
3. Liquidity tends to run out.
4. Return on investments won't.

PRICE'S LAWS:

1. If everybody doesn't want it, nobody gets it.

2. Mass man must be served by mass means.

3. Everything is contagious.

O'BRIEN'S LAW:

Nothing is ever done for the right reasons.

GLYME'S FORMULA FOR SUCCESS

The secret of success is sincerity. Once you can fake that you've got it made.

ADVANCED EXPERTSMANSHIP

MARS' RULE:

An expert is anyone from out of town.

WEBER'S DEFINITION:

An expert is one who knows more and more about less and less until he knows absolutely everything about nothing.

WARREN'S RULE:

To spot the expert, pick the one who predicts the job will take the longest and cost the most.

WINGER'S RULE:

If it sits on your desk for 15 minutes, you've just become the expert.

SCHROEDER'S LAW:

Indecision is the basis for flexibility.

GREEN'S LAW OF DEBATE:

Anything is possible if you don't know what you're talking about.

BURKE'S RULE:

Never create a problem for which you do not have the answer.

Corollary:

Create problems for which only you have the answer.

MATZ'S MAXIM:

A conclusion is the place where you got tired of thinking.

FAGIN'S RULE ON PAST PREDICTION:

Hindsight is an exact science.

FIRST RULE OF HISTORY:

History doesn't repeat itself — historians merely repeat each other.

DUNLAP'S LAWS OF PHYSICS:

1. Fact is solidified opinion.
2. Facts may weaken under extreme heat and pressure.
3. Truth is elastic.

MERKIN'S MAXIM:

When in doubt, predict that the trend will continue.

HALGREN'S SOLUTION:

When in trouble, obfuscate.

HAWKINS' THEORY OF PROGRESS:

Progress does not consist in replacing a theory that is wrong with one that is right. It consists in replacing a theory that is wrong with one that is more subtly wrong.

MEYER'S LAW:

It is a simple task to make things complex, but a complex task to make them simple.

HLADE'S LAW:

If you have a difficult task give it to a lazy man — he will find an easier way to do it.

HUNT'S LAW:

Every great idea has a disadvantage equal to or exceeding the greatness of the idea.

HANLON'S RAZOR:

Never attribute to malice that which is adequately explained by stupidity.

SYSTEMANTICS

In an age of mechasmic technological expansion and increasingly complex and alienating bureaucratic structures, a young physician and educator from Michigan has done much to help us understand the problems we must face if we are to survive this mess. John Gall, in his book *Systemantics* (N.Y., Quadrangle/N.Y. Times Book Co., 1977), draws upon advanced systems theory, modern organizational studies and timeless comic wisdom to construct his philosophy. A sampling:

THE FUNDAMENTAL THEOREM:

New systems generate new problems.

Corollary:
Systems should not be unnecessarily multiplied.

THE GENERALIZED UNCERTAINTY PRINCIPLE:

Systems tend to grow, and as they grow, they encroach.

Alternative Formulations:

1. Complicated systems produce unexpected outcomes.

2. The total behavior of large systems cannot be predicted.

Corollary: The Non-Additivity Theorem of Systems-Behavior

A large system, produced by expanding the dimensions of a smaller system, does not behave like the smaller system.

THE FUNCTIONARY'S FALSITY:

People in systems do not do what the system says they are doing.

THE OPERATIONAL FALLACY:

The system itself does not do what it says it is doing.

FIFTEENTH LAW OF SYSTEMANTICS:

A complex system that works is invariably found to have evolved from a simple system that works.

SIXTEENTH LAW OF SYSTEMANTICS:

A complex system designed from scratch never works and cannot be patched up to make it work. You have to start over, beginning with a working simple system.

THE FUNDAMENTAL POSTULATES OF ADVANCED SYSTEMS THEORY:

1. Everything is a system.

2. Everything is part of a larger system.

3. The universe is infinitely systematized, both upward (larger systems) and downward (smaller systems).

4. All systems are infinitely complex. (The illusion of simplicity comes from focussing attention on one or a few variables.)

LE CHATELIER'S PRINCIPLE:

Complex systems tend to oppose their own proper function.

ACADEMIOLOGY

LAWS OF CLASS SCHEDULING:

1. If the course you wanted most has room for 'n' students, you will be the 'n + 1' to apply.

2. Class schedules are designed so that every student will waste the maximum time between classes.

Corollary:
> When you are occasionally able to schedule two classes in a row, they will be held in classrooms at opposite ends of the campus.

3. A prerequisite for a desired course will be offered only during the semester following the desired course.

LAWS OF APPLIED TERROR:

1. When reviewing your notes before an exam, the most important ones will be illegible.

2. The more studying you did for the exam, the less sure you are as to which answer they want.

3. 80% of the final exam will be based on the one lecture you missed about the one book you didn't read.

4. The night before the English history mid-term, your Biology instructor will assign 200 pages on planaria.

Corollary:

Every instructor assumes that you have nothing else to do except study for that instructor's course.

5. If you are given an open-book exam, you will forget your book.

Corollary:
   If you are given a take-home exam, you will forget where you live.

6. At the end of the semester you will recall having enrolled in a course at the beginning of the semester — and never attending.

SEITS' LAW OF HIGHER EDUCATION:

The one course you must take to graduate will not be offered during your last semester.

ROMINGER'S RULES FOR STUDENTS:

1. The more general the title of a course, the less you will learn from it.

2. The more specific a title is, the less you will be able to apply it later.

DUGGAN'S LAW OF SCHOLARLY RESEARCH:

The most valuable quotation will be the one for which you cannot determine the source.

Corollary:
The source for an unattributed quotation will appear in the most hostile review of your work.

WHITTINGTON'S FIRST LAW OF COMMUNICATION:

When a writer prepares a manuscript on a subject he does not understand, his work will be understood only by readers who know more about that subject than he does.

Corollary:

Writings prepared without understanding must fail in the first objective of communication — informing the uninformed.

ROMINGER'S RULES FOR TEACHERS:

1. When a student asks for a second time if you have read his book report, he did not read the book.

2. If daily class attendance is mandatory, a scheduled exam will produce increased absenteeism. If attendance is optional, a scheduled exam will produce persons you have never seen before.

MEDICAL MURPHOLOGY

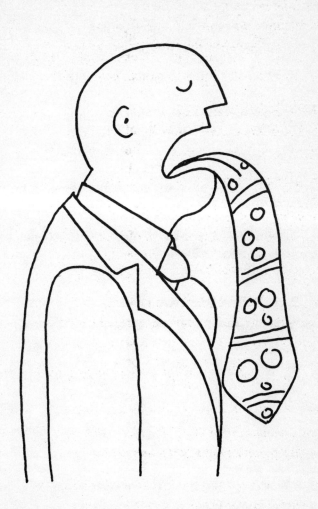

SIX PRINCIPLES FOR PATIENTS:

1. Just because your doctor has a name for your condition doesn't mean he knows what it is.

2. The more boring and out-of-date the magazines in the waiting room, the longer you will have to wait for your scheduled appointment.

3. Only adults have difficulty with child-proof bottles.

4. You never have the right number of pills left on the last day of a prescription.

5. The pills to be taken with meals will be the least appetizing ones.

   Corollary:
   Even water tastes bad when taken on doctor's orders.

6. If your condition seems to be getting better, it's probably your doctor getting sick.

MATZ'S WARNING:

Beware of the physician who is great at getting out of trouble.

MATZ'S RULE REGARDING MEDICATIONS:

A drug is that substance which, when injected into a rat, will produce a scientific report.

COCHRANE'S APHORISM:

Before ordering a test decide what you will do if it is 1) positive, or 2) negative. If both answers are the same, don't do the test.

BERNSTEIN'S PRECEPT:

The radiologists' national flower is the hedge.

LORD COHEN'S COMMENT:

The feasibility of an operation is not the best indication for its performance.

TELESCO'S LAWS OF NURSING:

1. All the IVs are at the other end of the hall.

2. A physician's ability is inversely proportional to his availability.

3. There are two kinds of adhesive tape: that which won't stay on and that which won't come off.

4. Everybody wants a pain shot at the same time.

5. Everybody who didn't want a pain shot when you were passing out pain shots wants one when you are passing out sleeping pills.

BARACH'S RULE:

An alcoholic is a person who drinks more than his own physician.

SPORTSMANSHIP-MANSHIP

WISE FAN'S LAMENT:

Fools rush in — and get the best seats.

BREDA'S RULE:

At any event, the people whose seats are furthest from the aisle arrive last.

MOSER'S LAW OF SPECTATOR SPORTS:

Exciting plays occur only while you are watching the scoreboard or out buying a hot dog.

MURRAY'S RULES OF THE ARENA:

1. Nothing is ever so bad it can't be made worse by firing the coach.
2. The wrong quarterback is the one that's in there.
3. A free agent is anything but.
4. Hockey is a game played by six good players and the home team.
5. Whatever can go to New York, will.

KNOX'S PRINCIPLE OF STAR QUALITY:

Whenever a superstar is traded to your favorite team, he fades. Whenever your team trades away a useless no-name, he immediately rises to stardom.

HERTZBERG'S FIRST LAW OF WING WALKING:

Never leave hold of what you've got until you've got hold of something else.

LAVIA'S LAW OF TENNIS:

A mediocre player will sink to the level of his or her opposition.

THE RULE OF THE RALLY:

The only way to make up for being lost is to make record time while you are lost.

DEAL'S LAWS OF SAILING:

1. The amount of wind will vary inversely with the number and experience of the people you take on board.

2. No matter how strong the breeze when you leave the dock, once you have reached the furthest point from port the wind will die.

PORKINGHAM'S LAWS OF SPORTFISHING:

1. The time available to go fishing shrinks as the fishing season draws nearer.

2. The least experienced fisherman always catches the biggest fish.

Corollary:

The more elaborate and costly the equipment, the greater the chance of having to stop at the fish market on the way home.

3. The worse your line is tangled, the better is the fishing around you.

MICHEHL'S RULE FOR PROSPECTIVE MOUNTAIN CLIMBERS:

The mountain gets steeper as you get closer.

Frothingham's Corollary:
The mountain looks closer than it is.

SHEDENHELM'S LAW OF BACKPACKING:

All trails have more uphill sections than they have level or downhill sections.

SMITH'S LAWS OF BRIDGE:

1. If your hand contains a singleton or a void, that is the suit your partner will bid . . . and bid . . . and bid . . .

2. If your hand contains the K, J, 9 of diamonds and the Ace of spades, when the dummy is spread to your left it will contain A, Q, 10 of diamonds and the King of spades.

3. The trump suit never breaks favorably when you are declarer.

THOMAS' LAW:

The one who least wants to play is the one who will win.

TODD'S FIRST LAW:

All things being equal, you lose.

Corollary:
All things being in your favor, you still lose.

JENSEN'S LAW:

Win or lose, you lose.

ROADSMANSHIP

OLIVER'S LAW OF LOCATION:

No matter where you go, there you are!

FIRST LAW OF TRAVEL:

It always takes longer to get there than to get back.

LAW OF LIFE'S HIGHWAY:

If everything is coming your way, you're in the wrong lane.

ATHENA'S RULES OF DRIVING COURTESY:

If you allow someone to get in front of you, either:

a) the car in front will be the last one over a railroad crossing, and you will be stuck waiting for a long, slow-moving train; or

b) you both will have the same destination, and the other car will get the last parking space.

LEMAR'S PARKING POSTULATE:

If you have to park six blocks away, you will find two new parking spaces right in front of the building entrance.

GRAY'S LAW FOR BUSES:

A bus that has refused to arrive will do so only when the would-be rider has walked to a point so close to the destination that it is no longer worthwhile to board the bus.

McKEE'S LAW:

When you're not in a hurry, the traffic light will turn green as soon as your vehicle comes to a complete stop.

QUIGLEY'S LAW:

A car and a truck approaching each other on an otherwise deserted road will meet at the narrow bridge.

REECE'S SECOND LAW:

The speed of an oncoming vehicle is directly proportional to the length of the passing zone.

DREW'S LAW OF HIGHWAY BIOLOGY:

The first bug to hit a clean windshield lands directly in front of your eyes.

CAMPBELL'S LAWS OF AUTOMOTIVE REPAIR:

1. If you can get to the faulty part, you don't have the tool to get it off.

2. If you can get the part off, the parts house will have it back-ordered.

3. If it's in stock, it didn't need replacing in the first place.

BROMBERG'S LAWS OF AUTOMOTIVE REPAIR:

1. When the need arises, any tool or object closest to you becomes a hammer.

2. No matter how minor the task, you will inevitably end up covered with grease and motor oil.

3. When necessary, metric and inch tools can be used interchangeably.

FEMO'S LAW OF AUTOMOTIVE ENGINE REPAIRING:

If you drop something, it will never reach the ground.

CONSUMEROLOGY & SALESMANSHIP

HERBLOCK'S LAW:

If it's good, they discontinue it.

GOLD'S LAW:

If the shoe fits, it's ugly.

HADLEY'S LAWS OF CLOTHING SHOPPING:

1. If you like it, they don't have it in your size.

2. If you like it and it's in your size, it doesn't fit anyway.

3. If you like it and it fits, you can't afford it.

4. If you like it, it fits and you can afford it, it falls apart the first time you wear it.

FINMAN'S BARGAIN BASEMENT PRINCIPLE:

The one you want is never the one on sale.

HERSHISER'S RULES:

1. Anything labeled "NEW" and/or "IMPROVED" isn't.

2. The label "NEW" and/or "IMPROVED" means the price went up.

3. The label "ALL NEW," "COMPLETELY NEW"or "GREAT NEW" means the price went way up.

McGOWAN'S MADISON AVENUE AXIOM:

If an item is advertised as "under $50," you can bet it's not $19.95.

LAW OF THE MARKETPLACE:

If only one price can be obtained for any quotation, the price will be unreasonable.

SINTETOS' FIRST LAW OF CONSUMERISM:

A 60-day warranty guarantees that the product will self-destruct on the 61st day.

BERYL'S LAW:

The "Consumer Report" on the item will come out a week after you've made your purchase.

Corollaries:

1. The one you bought will be rated "unacceptable."

2. The one you almost bought will be rated "best buy."

SAVIGNANO'S MAIL-ORDER LAW:

If you don't write to complain, you'll never receive your order.

If you do write, you'll receive the merchandise before your angry letter reaches its destination.

YOUNT'S LAWS OF MAIL ORDERING:

1. The most important item in an order will no longer be available.

2. The next most important item will be back-ordered for six months.

3. During the time an item is back-ordered, it will be available cheaper and quicker from many other sources.

4. As soon as a back-order has entered the "no longer available" category, the item will no longer be obtainable anywhere at any price.

LEWIS' LAW:

People will buy anything that's one to a customer.

BROOKS' LAWS OF RETAILING:

Security isn't.

Management can't.

Sale promotions don't.

Consumer assistance doesn't.

Workers won't.

HOUSEHOLD MURPHOLOGY

O'REILLY'S LAW OF THE KITCHEN:

Cleanliness is next to impossible.

SEVEN LAWS OF KITCHEN CONFUSION:

1. Multiple-function gadgets will not perform any function adequately.

Corollary:
The more expensive the gadget, the less often you will use it.

2. The simpler the instructions (e.g. "Press here"), the more difficult it will be to open the package.

3. In a family recipe you just discovered in an old book, the most vital measurement will be illegible.

Corollary:
You will discover that you can't read it only after you have mixed all the other ingredients.

4. Once a dish is fouled up, anything added to save it only makes it worse.

5. You are always complimented on the item which took the least effort to prepare.

Example:
If you make "duck a l'orange" you will be complimented on the baked potato.

6. The one ingredient you made a special trip to the store to get will be the one thing your guest is allergic to.

7. The more time and energy you put into preparing a meal, the greater the chance your guests will spend the entire meal discussing other meals they have had.

ALICE HAMMOND'S LAWS OF THE KITCHEN:

1. Souffles rise and cream whips only for the family and for guests you didn't really want to invite anyway.

2. The rotten egg will be the one you break into the cake batter. ·

3. Any cooking utensil placed in the dishwasher will be needed immediately thereafter for something else; any measuring utensil used for liquid ingredients will be needed immediately thereafter for dry ingredients.

4. Time spent consuming a meal is in inverse proportion to time spent preparing it.

5. Whatever it is, somebody will have had it for lunch.

WORKING COOK'S LAWS:

1. If you're wondering if you took the meat out to thaw, you didn't.

2. If you're wondering if you left the coffee pot plugged in, you did.

3. If you're wondering if you need to stop and pick up bread and eggs on the way home, you do.

4. If you're wondering if you have enough money to take the family out to eat tonight, you don't.

HAMILTON'S RULE FOR CLEANING
GLASSWARE:

The spot you are scrubbing is always on the other side.

Corollary:
If the spot is on the inside, you won't be able to reach it.

YEAGER'S LAW:

Washing machines only break down during the wash cycle.

Corollaries:
1. All break downs occur on the plumber's day off.

2. Cost of repair can be determined by multiplying the cost of your new coat by 1.75, or by multiplying the cost of a new washer by .75.

WALKER'S LAW OF THE HOUSEHOLD:

There is always more dirty laundry than clean laundry.

Clive's Rebuttal to Walker's Law:
If it's clean, it isn't laundry.

SKOFF'S LAW:

A child will not spill on a dirty floor.

VAN ROY'S LAW:

An unbreakable toy is useful for breaking other toys.

WITZLING'S LAWS OF PROGENY PERFORMANCE:

1. Any child who chatters non-stop at home will adamantly refuse to utter a word when requested to demonstrate for an audience.

2. Any shy, introverted child will choose a crowded public area to loudly demonstrate newly acquired vocabulary (damn, penis, etc.).

C. H. FISH'S LAWS OF ANIMAL BEHAVIOR:

1. The probability of a cat eating its dinner has absolutely nothing to do with the price of the food placed before it.

2. The probability that a household pet will raise a fuss to go in or out is directly proportional to the number and importance of your dinner guests.

FISKE'S TEENAGE COROLLARY TO PARKINSON'S LAW:

The stomach expands to accommodate the amount of junk food available.

BANANA PRINCIPLE:

If you buy bananas or avocados before they are ripe, there won't be any left by the time they are ripe. If you buy them ripe, they rot before they are eaten.

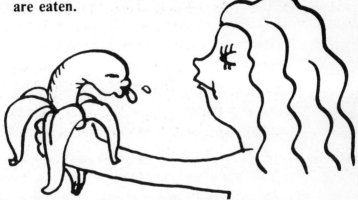

BALLANCE'S LAW OF RELATIVITY:

How long a minute is depends on which side of the bathroom door you're on.

BRITT'S GREEN THUMB POSTULATE:

The life expectancy of a house plant varies inversely with its price and directly with its ugliness.

LAW OF RERUNS:

If you have watched a TV series only once, and you watch it again, it will be a rerun of the same episode.

JONES' LAWS OF TV PROGRAMMING:

1. If there are only two shows worth watching, they will be on at the same time.

2. The only new show worth watching will be cancelled.

3. The show you've been looking forward to all week will be preempted.

BESS' UNIVERSAL PRINCIPLES:

1. The telephone will ring when you are outside the door, fumbling for your keys.

2. You will reach it just in time to hear the click of the caller hanging up.

KOVAC'S CONUNDRUM:

When you dial a wrong number, you never get a busy signal.

RYAN'S APPLICATION OF PARKINSON'S LAW:

Possessions increase to fill the space available for their storage.

SOCIO-MURPHOLOGY (HUMANSHIP)

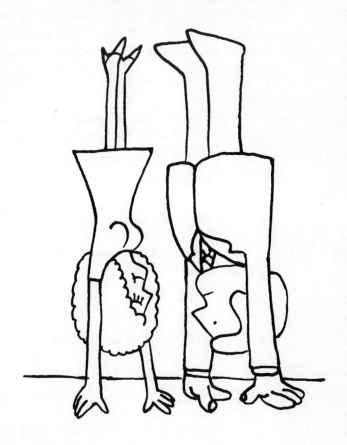

SHIRLEY'S LAW:

Most people deserve each other.

ARTHUR'S LAWS OF LOVE:

1. People to whom you are attracted invariably think you remind them of someone else.

2. The love letter you finally got the courage to send will be delayed in the mail long enough for you to make a fool of yourself in person.

3. Other people's romantic gestures seem novel and exciting.
   Your own romantic gestures seem foolish and clumsy.

THOMS' LAW OF MARITAL BLISS:

The length of a marriage is inversely proportional to the amount spent on the wedding.

BEDFELLOW'S RULE:

The one who snores will fall asleep first.

GILLENSON'S (de-sexed) LAWS OF EXPECTATION:

1. Never get excited about a blind date because of how it sounds over the phone.

2. Never get excited about a person because of what it looks like from behind.

COLVARD'S LOGICAL PREMISES:

All probabilities are 50%. Either a thing will happen or it won't.

Colvard's Unconscionable Commentary:
This is especially true when dealing with women.

Grelb's Commentary on Colvard's Premise:
Likelihoods, however, are 90% against you.

FARMER'S CREDO:

Sow your wild oats on Saturday night — then on Sunday pray for crop failure.

RUBY'S PRINCIPLE OF CLOSE ENCOUNTERS:

The probability of meeting someone you know increases when you are with someone you don't want to be seen with.

CHEIT'S LAMENT:

If you help a friend in need, he is sure to remember you — the next time he's in need.

DENNISTON'S LAW:

Virtue is its own punishment.

Denniston's Corollary:
If you do something right once, someone will ask you to do it again.

Bloch's Commentary:
Denniston's Corollary properly applies to the statement: "Virtuous action will never go unpunished." Denniston's Law has much broader implications.

MASON'S FIRST LAW OF SYNERGISM:

The one day you'd sell your soul for something, souls are a glut.

RON'S OBSERVATIONS FOR TEENAGERS:

1. The pimples don't appear until the hour before the date.

2. The scratch on the record is always through the song you like most.

UNDERLYING PRINCIPLE OF SOCIO-GENETICS:

Superiority is recessive.

PROFESSOR BLOCK'S MOTTO:

Forgive and remember.

PARDO'S FIRST POSTULATE (from *Murphy's Law*):

Anything good in life is either illegal, immoral or fattening.

STEINKOPFF'S EXTENSION TO PARDO'S FIRST POSTULATE:

(The good things in life also) . . . cause cancer in laboratory mice and are taxed beyond reality.

JACOBS' LAW:

To err is human — to blame it on someone else is even more human.

EDELSTEIN'S ADVICE:

Don't worry over what other people are thinking about you. They're too busy worrying over what you are thinking about them.

MEADER'S LAW:

Whatever happens to you, it will previously have happened to everyone you know, only more so.

BOCKLAGE'S LAW:

He who laughs last — probably didn't get the joke.

META-LAWS

DIGIOVANNI'S LAW:

The number of Laws will expand to fill the publishing space available.

LEO ROGERS' BLESSING FOR VOLUME II:

If it's worth doing, it's worth overdoing.

ROGERS' OBSERVATION REGARDING THE LAWS:

In a bureaucratic hierarchy, the higher up the organization the less people appreciate Murphy's Law, the Peter Principle, etc.

OAKS' PRINCIPLES OF LAWMAKING:

1. Law expands in proportion to the resources available for its enforcement.
2. Bad law is more likely to be supplemented than repealed.
3. Social legislation cannot repeal physical laws.

JAFFE'S PRECEPT:

There are some things which are impossible to know — but it is impossible to know these things.

MUIR'S LAW:

When we try to pick out anything by itself we find it hitched to everything else in the universe.

DUCHARM'S AXIOM:

If one views his problem closely enough he will recognize himself as part of the problem.

LAW OF ARBITRARY DISTINCTION:

Anything may be divided into as many parts as you please.

Corollary:

Everything may be divided into as many parts as you please.

Commentary on the Corollary:

In this case, 'everything' may be viewed as a subset of 'anything.'

THE LAST LAW:

If several things that could have gone wrong have not gone wrong, it would have been ultimately beneficial for them to have gone wrong.

This book is published by

PRICE/STERN/SLOAN
Publishers, Inc., Los Angeles

whose other splendid titles titles include such literary classics as:

**MURPHY'S LAW AND OTHER REASONS
WHY THINGS GO WRONG! ($2.95)**

HOW TO BE A JEWISH MOTHER ($2.95)

LEGAL GUIDE TO MOTHER GOOSE ($2.50)

HOW TO BE AN ITALIAN ($2.95)

THE PROFIT ($2.50)

ART AFTERPIECES ($3.95)

W.C. FIELDS SPEAKS ($2.75)

INCREDIBLE INSURANCE CLAIMS ($2.95)

and many, many more

They are available wherever books are sold, or may
be ordered directly from the publisher by sending
check or money order for total amount plus $1.00
for handling and mailing. For complete list of
titles send *stamped, self-addressed envelope* to:

PRICE/STERN/SLOAN   *Publishers, Inc.*
410 North La Cienega Boulevard, Los Angeles, California 90048

pss!®